D0794272

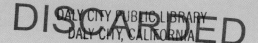
From the Arctic to Antarctica

R od Theodorou

Heinemann Library
Chicago, Illinois

©2000 Reed Educational & Professional Publishing
Published by Heinemann Library,
an imprint of Reed Educational & Professional Publishing,
100 N. LaSalle, Suite 1010
Chicago, IL 60602
Customer Service 888-454-2279

Designed by **AMR**
Illustrated by Art Construction, Stephen Lings at Linden Artists and Darrell Warner at Beehive Illustration.
Printed by Wing King Tong, in Hong Kong

04 03 02 01 00
10 9 8 7 6 5 4 3 2 1

Library of Congress Cataloging-in-Publication Data
Theodorou, Rod.
    From the Arctic to Antarctica / Rod Theodorou.
        p. cm. --(Amazing journeys)
    Includes bibliographical references.
    Summary: Investigates the physical features of the North and South
Poles, arctic and antarctic life, weather and light conditions, and
conservation efforts.
    ISBN 1-57572-485-5 (library binding)
    1. Natural history--Polar regions Juvenile literature.
[1. Natural history--Polar regions. 2. Polar regions.] I. Title.
II. Series: Telford, Carole, 1961– Amazing journeys.
QH84.1.T54 2000
508.311--dc21   99-37160
                                             CIP

Acknowledgments

The Publishers would like to thank the following for permission to reproduce photographs:

BBC/Bernard Walton, p. 17; BBC/Jessie Lane, p. 25; BBC/Mats Forberg, p. 13; BBC/Mike Potts, p. 17; British Antarctic Survey/J. Coleman, p. 19; Oxford Scientific Films, p. 13; Oxford Scientific Films/Ben Osborne, p. 25; Oxford Scientific Films/Bob Gibbons, p. 17; Oxford Scientific Films/C. J. Gilbert, p. 21; Oxford Scientific Films/Colin Monteath, pp. 24, 27; Oxford Scientific Films/David C Fritts, p. 14; Oxford Scientific Films/Doug Allan, pp.11, 19, 21, 22, 23; Oxford Scientific Films/Howard Hall, p. 10; Oxford Scientific Films/Norbert Rosing, p. 15; Oxford Scientific Films/Peter Hawkley p. 23; Tom Ulrich, p. 15; Oxford Scientific Films/Tui de Roy p. 6; Science Photo Library/Vanessa Vick, p. 26.

Cover photograph reproduced with permission of Planet Earth Pictures.

Every effort has been made to contact copyright holders of any material reproduced in this book. Any omissions will be rectified in subsequent printings if notice is given to the Publisher.

Some words are shown in bold, **like this.**
You can find out what they mean by looking in the glossary.

Contents

Introduction

You are about to go on an amazing journey. You are going to follow in the footsteps of the great explorers to discover two of the coldest, wildest, and most **isolated** places on Earth. You are going to travel to the Arctic and Antarctica.

You will travel from the very depths of the freezing ocean, up onto **permanently** frozen lands covered in thick ice. You will discover how each part of the sea and land is home to amazing animals and plants. Each living thing has its own special way to survive in these hard and hostile conditions at Earth's **polar** regions.

Antarctica and areas of the Arctic are permanently frozen and covered with ice.

The Arctic is actually a huge frozen ocean around the **North Pole**. Antarctica is an enormous **continent** on which the **South Pole** is located. When it is winter in the Arctic, it is summer in Antarctica. When it is winter in Antarctica, it is summer in the Arctic. During the long winter months, there are blizzards and freezing temperatures at both places. Average winter temperatures are −22° F (−30 °C) in the Arctic and −76° F (−60° C) in Antarctica. There is constant darkness in winter because the sun is shining at the other pole. When summer comes, the sun's rays melt some of the ice and snow. Many animals **migrate** to the area in the summer to feed, **mate**, and raise their young.

As Earth turns, the pole facing toward the sun is in summer, while the other pole is in winter darkness.

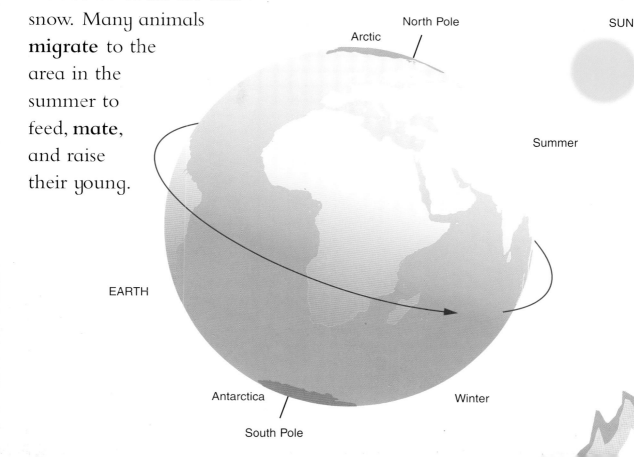

North Pole

Arctic

SUN

Summer

EARTH

Antarctica

South Pole

Winter

Journey Map

Here are two maps showing the **polar** regions we are going to explore. We are going to start in a **submersible**, deep under the sea. We will rise to the surface and walk onto the ice sheet above it. We will then travel by **snowmobile** across the ice of the Arctic and Antarctica.

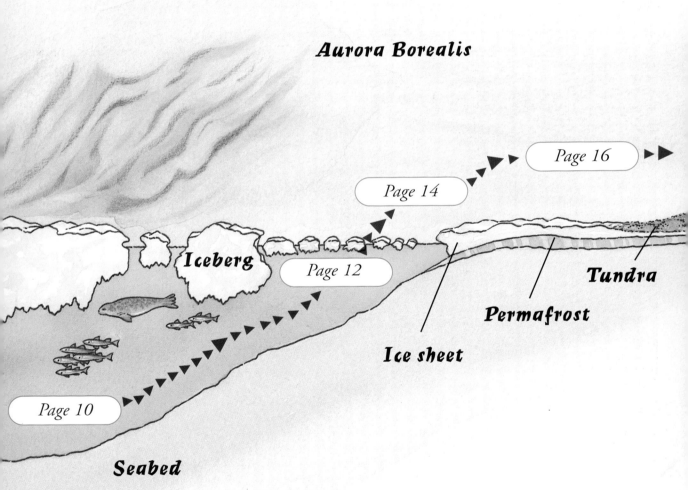

Aurora Borealis

Page 16 ▶▶

Page 14

Page 12

Iceberg

Page 10

Tundra

Permafrost

Ice sheet

Seabed

ARCTIC

The polar regions are made up of layers of frozen ice. Some parts of these ice sheets are thought to be 200,000 years old. As more and more snow pushes down onto this ice, some of the ice begins to move slowly downward toward the sea. This kind of ice sheet is called a **glacier**. Wind and waves break some of this ice off and it floats in the water as huge **icebergs**.

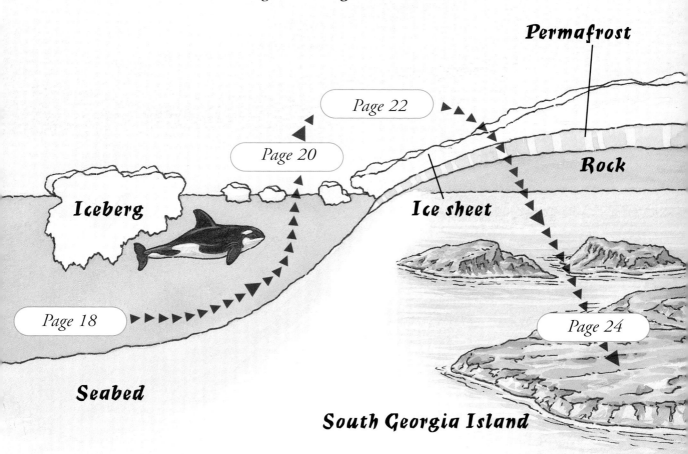

Permafrost

Page 22

Page 20

Rock

Iceberg

Ice sheet

Page 18

Page 24

Seabed

South Georgia Island

ANTARCTICA

The Arctic
Up from the Depths

Our journey begins in a **submersible** on the seabed of the Arctic Ocean. It is cold and dark. We can hardly see anything through our **portholes** until something swims right past. Beneath us on the seabed are brittlestars and sea urchins, living amid the broken-down remains of dead animals and dead **plankton**.

We hope to catch sight of a sperm whale. All whales are **mammals**. They have to come to the surface of the sea to breathe, but sperm whales can hold their breath and dive as deep as 3,200 feet (1,000 meters)! Here in the icy ocean depths, they fight huge battles with their **prey**, giant squid. The battles can leave the whales covered in scars, made by squid suckers.

Sperm whales have an enormous and strange-looking **snout**. It is full of liquid wax, called spermaceti oil, which helps the whales sink down into the depths to hunt.

Beluga whale

The beluga, or white whale, is one of the few animals that can live in the cold of the Arctic Ocean all year round. Most belugas choose to stay for the summer only, when they can feast on the **polar** cod, haddock, and other fish.

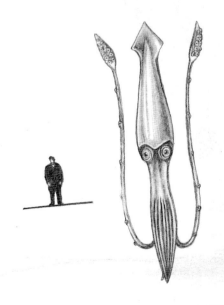

Narwhal

The narwhal, like the beluga and sperm whale, is a toothed whale that swims with others in a **pod**. The whales in the pod communicate by making whistles and clicks through their **blowholes.**

Giant squid

Giant squid are huge and mysterious creatures that live deep down near the bottom of the ocean. No one has ever seen one alive, but remains of these animals have been found on beaches.

At the Pack Ice

As we reach the surface and the edge of the **pack-ice** shelf, we open the hatch on top of the **submersible**. The air is icy and fresh. We can see and hear a wealth of animal life around us, making the most of the Arctic summer. Although it is summer, it is very cold here, and we are surrounded by ice. The ice floating on the sea's surface is only a few feet thick, but dotted around us are massive **icebergs**. Icebergs are chunks of ice that have broken off the main ice sheet and floated away. They will gradually break up and melt, but this process can take two to three years. Big icebergs can be dangerous to ships. Only a small part of the iceberg shows at the surface of the sea—most is hidden underwater.

The moving **glacier** has made a platform of ice that stretches out from the main ice sheet.

1. little auk
2. harp seal
3. eider duck
4. ringed seal
5. ringed seal lair
6. walrus
7. plankton
8. puffin
9. iceberg
10. glacier

Ringed seal

The female uses her teeth and flippers to scrape funnel-shaped tunnels through the ice to reach breathing holes at the surface. She will give birth to her pups in the safety and warmth of her **lair**.

Plankton

Plankton are tiny plants and animals that can be found in all seas. They float near the surface of the sea, soaking up the sun's rays, which help them to grow. Plankton are very important because they are the basic food for many animals, both large and small.

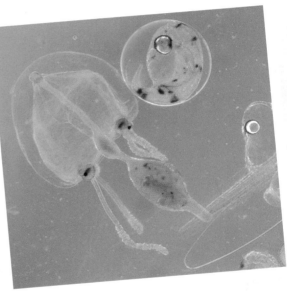

Walrus

Walruses spend their time hunting in the sea or resting on the ice. They have **tusks** that can be up to 3 feet (0.9 meters) long. They use them to dig up shellfish from the seabed.

On the Ice Sheet

It is time to leave the **submersible** and jump down onto the ice covering the land farthest north. Although it is nighttime now, the sun has not set. There is something strange above us. The sky is full of bright trails of brilliant light. These are the northern lights, or *Aurora Borealis.* These lights show when energy from the sun reacts with gases in Earth's **polar** atmosphere, making the gases give off wispy trails of colored light.

Be careful and stand very still! Something else has been drawn to the lights. Prowling quietly ahead of us is the "King of the Arctic"—the polar bear. Once it has passed by, we must escape by **snowmobile** and speed inland to the **tundra**.

During the Arctic summer months, the sun never sets. The Arctic is sometimes called the "land of the midnight sun."

Ptarmigan

This hardy bird lives in the Arctic all year round. It is white in winter, so it blends with the ice and is hidden from its **prey** and from **predators**. In the summer, its feathers change to a brownish color.

Polar bear

This is the largest bear in the world. The male is almost twice as tall as the average human male and ten times as heavy. Polar bears have good eyesight, a good sense of smell, and sharp claws, all of which help them to hunt.

White hunter

Polar bears eat birds, fish, and plants, but their favorite food is ringed seal. A bear will lie quietly next to a seal's breathing hole for hours, covering its black nose with its white paw. When the seal pops its head out of the hole, the bear grabs it and kills it with its paws and teeth.

Across the Tundra

We have reached some land on an Arctic island. It is **tundra**, a flat, treeless region where the ice melts during the brief summer **thaw**. The ground is wet, boggy soil, and a little below the surface is a frozen layer called **permafrost**.

The temperature has risen, but only to 45° F (7° C)! This is warm enough for mosses, lichen, and small bushes to grow. Insects have emerged and buzz in the air. Herds of animals have **migrated** here to enjoy a feeding and **mating** season that will last six to eight weeks, or until the summer ends. It is time to plan our next amazing journey south to experience what life is like in summer in Antarctica.

1. mosquitoes
2. skuas
3. butterflies
4. grizzly bear
5. gray wolf
6. musk oxen
7. snow geese
8. caribou
9. snowshoe hare
10. Arctic fox
11. moose
12. Arctic willow
13. northern fleabane
14. golden eagle
15. reindeer moss
16. snowy owl
17. lemmings
18. mosses and lichens

In summer, thousands of animals migrate to the Arctic tundra from farther south.

Caribou

Caribou are American reindeer. In summer, thousands of them trek north over familiar routes, from forests on the edges of the Arctic, up to their summer **breeding** ground in the tundra.

Northern fleabane

This plant flowers during the Arctic summer. Fleas and **midges** hate its taste, which is how it got its name. Humans can use it as an insect repellent.

Lemmings

Lemmings are **rodents** that spend a lot of their lives sheltering in burrows under the ground. If they come out into the open in summer, larger animals such as snowy owls and golden eagles hunt and eat them.

ANTARCTICA
Deep-Sea Approach

We have completed our long journey to Antarctica and are now resting on the seabed in a **submersible**. We begin the ascent to the surface. As the dark water begins to get brighter, we realize that there is an amazing amount of sea life down here. The animals at the bottom feed on each other, or on dead **plankton** that fall from the surface. As we rise up into the mid-water, we see huge **schools** of fish. There is plenty of food for such fish-eating **predators** as penguins and seals. Penguins and seals serve as food for even larger Antarctic predators, such as leopard seals and orcas, or killer whales. Killer whales hunt in packs of up to twelve and are usually led by a large male.

1. anemones
2. sponges
3. starfish
4. sea spider
5. sea urchin
6. killer whale
7. cod
8. Ross seal
9. krill

The ocean around Antarctica is rich in sea life.

Sponge

There are approximately 300 varieties of sponges in the Antarctic Ocean. Some of them can live for several hundred years.

Starfish

Antarctic starfish are bright red. They have special tube-like feet with which they grasp their **prey**, once they have located it by smell. Antarctic starfish can live for many years on the seabed.

Sea anemones

Sea anemones look like blobs of jelly, but they have strong **tentacles** with special organs that can paralyze their prey, such as small fish or starfish. They also use their tentacles to push the prey into their mouth opening.

At the Sea's Edge

As we reach the sea's surface and the edge of the continent, the first thing that strikes us is the number of seals! There are millions of them **breeding** in **colonies** all along the ice-covered coast. There are Weddell seals, which can dive for over an hour hunting for fish. There are Ross seals, silver-coated crabeater seals, and ferocious leopard seals. The largest are elephant seals, including a few gigantic fighting males. Elephant seals were hunted almost to **extinction** in the nineteenth century. The largest group of seals is the crabeaters. This is a safe breeding ground for them with plenty of food in the sea. There can be up to 30 million of them living in the sea or on the floating ice!

1. icefish
2. Antarctic cod
3. albatross
4. Ross seal
5. leopard seal
6. crabeater seal
7. Weddell seal
8. Adélie penguins
9. elephant seal

Vast colonies of seals and penguins live on the Antarctic **pack ice**.

Antarctic icefish

The Antarctic icefish is sometimes called the antifreeze fish because it has special **molecules** in its body that keep its blood and other fluids from freezing in the icy Antarctic seas.

Krill

Krill are small, shrimplike creatures that are about 2 inches (5 centimeters) long. In winter, they live under the pack ice eating algae and **plankton**. In summer they appear in huge numbers and are food for the whales, penguins, and seals.

Leopard seal

Leopard seals are terrifying **predators**. They hunt fish, penguins, and other seals. Sometimes they creep up on a penguin underneath the ice, then smash up through the ice to catch it.

On the Ice Sheet

At last we have reached the Antarctic ice sheet, the coldest place on Earth. Many animals battle for food around the edge of the ice sheet. It is very noisy and very cold. We are surrounded on all sides by penguins, the most famous residents.

Penguins are birds that cannot fly, but their wings and streamlined shape make them excellent swimmers. They can stay underwater for up to eighteen minutes, steering with their feet and swimming with their strong wings. They catch fish, squid, and krill to eat. In the summer, they come ashore to their nesting sites to lay their eggs and feed their young.

One parent stays with the egg while the other goes to sea to feed. Three weeks after hatching, the chicks join other chicks in nursery groups. They stay together, while the adults search for food.

The most common Antarctic penguin is the Adélie penguin.

22

Arctic tern

The Arctic tern **mates** in the far north in the northern summer, then **migrates** to Antarctica for the summer. It migrates farther than any other bird.

Emperor penguin

The female lays a single egg in autumn. She gives it to the male to keep it warm in a roll of fat above his feet. The males huddle together, while the females go to sea to feed for two months. The males eat nothing during this time. The chicks hatch in the dead of winter, and the females return, fat and healthy, to tend them. The very hungry males finally get to go off and eat.

Skua

Skuas are large, aggressive gulls with sharp, hooked beaks. They nest near penguin **colonies** so that they can steal and eat penguin chicks and eggs.

Antarctic Islands

We are now at the final stage of our journey. We have crossed the sea to one of the islands off the coast of Antarctica. During the summer, islands like South Georgia are green and mostly free of snow. The island's small lakes have **thawed** a little and will remain thawed for a month or two. Every year, about 300,000 seals come here to find food and **mate.** As we reach the beaches, we can see thousands of these seals. The noise is deafening.

As the winter draws near, even these animals will begin to **migrate** to warmer places. Here, we too must end our amazing journey.

South Georgia is an island that has more open land in summer than the continent does.

Elephant seals

The elephant seal is the largest seal. It can reach up to 20 feet (6 meters) long. The males have big trunklike noses. They fight great battles over the smaller females.

Albatross

The wandering albatross has the biggest wingspan of all birds—as much as 12 feet (3.6 meters)! It uses its huge wings to catch the strong sea winds and be carried at speeds of 50 miles (80 kilometers) an hour!

Nesting giants

Thousands of albatross **breed** on South Georgia Island. After finding food for the chick, the adults return to the nest. The chick taps on the adult's beak, making it let the food come back up its throat for the chick to eat.

Conservation and the Future

At risk

As our plane takes off from Antarctica, we see the spectacular **continent** lying below us, almost untouched by human existence. However, both the Arctic and the Antarctic are at risk from human **pollution** and hunting, and must be protected if the animal and plant life is to continue to thrive.

Many species of animals have been hunted over the years for their skins or for food. Such animals as polar bears, seals, and whales have faced **extinction**. Most are now protected. Fishing limits have also been set to prevent vast numbers of krill, squid, and fish from being caught, damaging the **food chain**.

The 1989 *Exxon Valdez* oil spill off Alaska polluted life in the cold Arctic sea.

Pollution

Pollution has also harmed life at the poles. Pollution from oil spills, **radiation** from nuclear power plants, and waste from industry have damaged many stretches of **polar** coastline.

The Arctic has already suffered, but in 1991, 40 countries agreed to protect Antarctica during the next 50 years. Industry is limited, and tourists can visit only in a few organized groups. It is important that these areas be conserved for future generations to study and enjoy. We can all work to preserve these amazing unspoiled lands so that one day our children can come here and enjoy their own amazing journeys.

Few tourist trips are allowed in Antarctic waters.

27

Glossary

breed, breeding	refers to place where animals produce babies or the process of producing and raising the babies
blowhole	opening in the top of a whale's head for breathing air
colonies	groups of similar things living together
continent	one of the seven large areas of land that make up the world
extinction	permanent disappearance of a kind of animal or plant
food chain	natural system in which smaller animals are eaten by bigger animals, who are eaten by even bigger animals
glacier	sheet of ice that moves slowly across land
iceberg	large piece of ice floating in the sea
isolated	lonely or far away from other things
lair	place where an animal lives or hides
mammals	warm-blooded animals, such as humans, that have hair and feed their young on their mother's milk
mate	of a male and female, to join to produce babies
midge	tiny fly
migrate	to move from one place to another, often to feed or mate
molecule	very small part of a chemical
North Pole	most northern part of Earth
pack ice	sea ice that has been crushed into one big mass
permafrost	ice beneath the soil that remains frozen even in summer when the soil thaws

permanently	always
plankton	tiny animal and plant life that floats or swims in water
pod	large group of whales living together
polar	occurring near the North Pole or the South Pole
pollution	something that makes air, water, or soil dirty
porthole	window in the side of a ship
predator	animal that hunts, kills, and eats other animals
prey	animals that are hunted by predators
radiation	energy that moves out from the source in waves
rodent	small mammal with gnawing front teeth, such as a mouse, squirrel, or rat
school	large group of the same type of fish
snout	animal's nose
snowmobile	motor vehicle on skis for traveling on snow and ice
South Pole	most southern part of Earth
submersible	underwater craft used for deep-sea research
tentacle	long and flexible part of some animals that is used to feel or touch
thaw	to melt
tundra	flat, treeless area in the Arctic with a layer of ice beneath the soil
tusk	big tooth that sticks out of an animal's mouth, even when it is closed

More Books to Read

Baines, John D. *Antarctica*. Austin, Tex.: Raintree Steck-Vaughn, 1997.

Blashfield, Jean F. *Antarctica*. Austin, Tex.: Raintree Steck-Vaughn, 1995.

Forman, Michael H. *An Arctic Tundra*. Danbury, Conn.: Children's Press, 1997.

Fowler, Allan. *Arctic Tundra: Land with No Trees*. Danbury, Conn.: Children's Press, 1996.

Inseth, Zachary. *The Tundra*. Chanhassen, Minn.: The Child's World, Inc., 1998.

McCurdy, Michael. *Trapped by the Ice!: Shackleton's Amazing Antarctic Adventure*. New York: Walker & Co., 1997.

Stone, Lynn M. *The Antarctic*. Vero Beach, Fla.: Rourke Corporation, 1996.

—. *Antarctica: The Land*. Vero Beach, Fla.: Rourke Book Company, Inc., 1995.

Organizations

Cousteau Society
870 Greenbrier Circle
Suite 402
Chesapeake, Va. 23320
Tel. (800) 441-4395

Earthwatch Institute U.S.
680 Mount Auburn Street
Watertown, Mass. 02471
Tel. (800) 776-0188

Greenpeace U.S.A.
1436 U Street N.W
Washington, D.C. 20009
Tel. (202) 462-1177

National Wildlife Federation
8925 Leesburg Pike
Vienna, Va. 22184
Tel. (703) 790-4100

Save the Whales
PO Box 2397
Venice, CA 90291

Index